The Big Day!
Going to Hospital

Nicola Barber

WAYLAND

First published in 2008 by Wayland

Copyright © Wayland 2008

Wayland
338 Euston Road
London NW1 3BH

Wayland Australia
Level 17/207 Kent Street
Sydney, NSW 2000

Editor: Camilla Lloyd
Designer: Elaine Wilkinson
Picture Researcher: Kathy Lockley

Picture Acknowledgments: The author and publisher would like to thank the following for their pictures to be reproduced in this publication: Cover photograph: LWA-JDC/Corbis; Charles Thatcher/Stone/Getty Images: 7; Colin Gray/Photonica/Getty Images: 21; Corbis: 16, 24; Doable/Acollection/Getty Images: 20; Duncan Raban/Great Ormond Street Hospital for Children: 8, 13; Great Ormond Street Hospital for Children: 11; Janine Wiedel Photo Library/Alamy Images: 15; Jeff Kaufman/Taxi/Getty Images: 6; Jennie Woodcock/Bubbles Photolibrary: 17; John Birdsall/John Birdsall Social Issues Photo Library: 9, 19; LWA-JDC/Corbis: 18; Peter Dazeley/Photographer's Choice/Getty Images: 14; Photofusion Picture Library: 1, 12; Picture Partners/Alamy Images: 10; Randy Faris/Corbis: 5.

Photographs reproduced with the kind permission of Duncan Raban and Great Ormond Street Hospital for Children, London.

British Library Cataloguing in Publication Data:
Barber, Nicola
   Going to hospital. - (The big day)
   1. Hospitals - Juvenile literature
   I. Title
   362.1'1

ISBN: 978 0 7502 5363 5

Printed in China

Wayland is a division of Hachette Children's Books, an Hachette Livre UK company

Contents

Feeling unwell

It's not much fun feeling unwell.
When your throat is sore, or your
head hurts, you don't feel like doing much.

What happens when you don't feel well?

When you are ill you don't go to school.
You stay at home so that your Mum or
Dad can look after you.

Seeing the doctor

Sometimes when you are ill your parents take you to see a doctor. Usually you go to see the doctor at your local surgery.

But sometimes you might have to go
to hospital to see a different doctor,
or to have some tests.

At the hospital

Hospitals are often
big and busy places,
with lots of people.
All the nurses and
doctors wear
badges with their
names on.

You might only
stay in the hospital
for a few hours.
If you have to
stay for longer
you will be
given a special
bracelet with
your name
on it.

Staying overnight

Sometimes you might need to stay in the hospital for a while.

If you are going to stay overnight you will need to pack your night clothes, your toothbrush and a special toy for company.

You could take a few of your favourite games or books. Usually your Mum or Dad will stay in the hospital with you to help the nurses look after you.

On the ward

A nurse will show you where your bed is.
You might be in a room on your own,
or you might be sharing a room with several
other children. This is called a ward.

Most children's wards have a playroom,
full of toys and things to do. You can eat
your meals in the ward, and you might even
have your own TV by your bed.

Finding out what's wrong

Hospitals have lots of
equipment and machines
to help doctors and nurses
find out why you are ill.
Some machines listen to
your heart beating or
measure your temperature.

Other machines take pictures of your
bones. The doctor might need to take
some of your blood to check it.

Having an operation

You might need an operation to make you feel better. You will probably have to wear a special gown that does up at the back. You won't be able to have anything to eat or drink for a while before the operation – you'll probably feel hungry!

The doctor will give you an injection
to make you sleep during the operation.
Afterwards, the nurse will tell you when
you can start to drink and eat again.

Visitors

Your family and friends can come to visit you while you are in hospital.

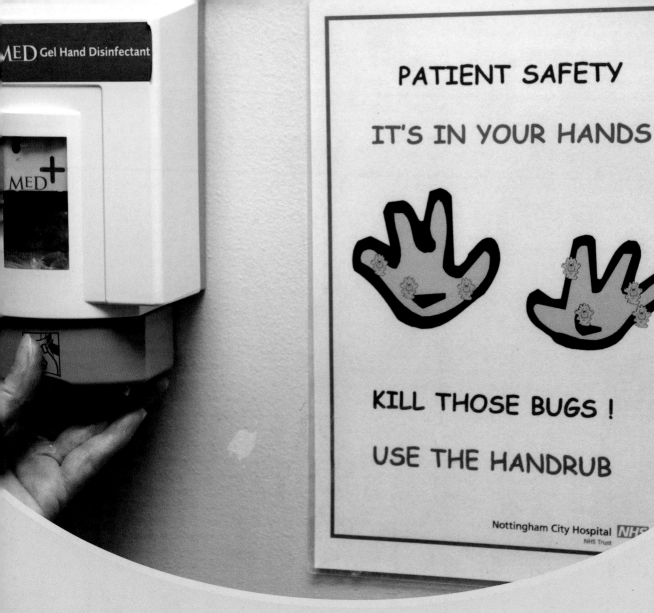

Before they come into the ward, everyone must wash their hands with special soap to make sure they are clean. Some wards have a doorbell, so a nurse can let people in.

Going home

When you are well enough it is time to go home. You can say goodbye to your friends at the hospital. Sometimes you will take some medicine home with you.

Later, you might need to go back to the hospital for a short visit so the doctor can check you are completely better.

Get well soon!

Hospital words

If you are writing about going to hospital, these are some of the words you might need to use.

Badge

Blood

Bracelet

Doctor

Gown

Ill

Injection

Medicine

Nurse

Operation

Surgery

Temperature

Ward

Further information

Books

Going to the Hospital (Usborne First Experiences)
by Anna Civardi, Usborne Books, 2005

I Don't Want to go to Hospital (A Little Princess Story)
by Tony Ross, Picture Lions 2001

My First Visit to Hospital (First Times) by Rebecca Hunter,
Evans Brothers, 2005

Topsy and Tim Go to Hospital by Jean and Gareth Adamson,
Ladybird Books, 2003

Website for children

http://www.kidshealth.org/kid/feel_better/places/hospital.html

Websites for parents

http://www.childrenfirst.nhs.uk/families/hospital/index.html

http://www.gosh.nhs.uk/gosh_families/coming_to_gosh/index.html

http://www.actionforsickchildren.org/parentshospital.html

Index